# Team Empowerment

## 20 Ways to Get There

### Volume 6 of The Parker Team Series

"Empowerment is an essential ingredient of a successful cross-functional team. And it's importance extends to just about every type and manner of team, including those composed of scientists, technical professionals, service staff, administrative people, and even managers."

– Glenn Parker

## GLENN PARKER

HRD Press, Inc. • Amherst • Massachusetts

Published by:    HRD Press, Inc.
22 Amherst Road
Amherst, MA 01002
1-800-822-2801 (U.S. and Canada)
413-253-3488
413-253-3490 (fax)
www.hrdpress.com

ISBN 978-1-59996-200-9

Editorial Services: Robert W. Carkhuff
Production Services: Jean S. Miller
Cover Design: Eileen Klockars

# EMPOWERMENT Is...

Let's begin with the basics:

*An empowered team is one that has both the responsibility and authority to carry out its mission and exercises its ownership and control over its task and resources.*

— Glenn Parker, *Cross-Functional Teams,*
2nd Ed., Jossey-Bass/Wiley, 2003

As this definition makes clear, empowerment is all about boundaries; it is not *carte blanche!*

In a practical sense, it means that a group of people can make decisions about certain aspects of their work *without checking with anyone.*

A team can be empowered by management as in the case of a project team that was told by senior management, "here is your goal, here is your budget, here are the other resources you may utilize, you are empowered to make the decisions necessary to achieve that goal within the parameters of this budget." However, a team can also empower themselves in the absence of any organizational prohibitions to the contrary; a team may take the initiative to "go for it."

As long as their actions are legal, ethical, compatible with company policy and in the best interests of the organization and the customer, I advise teams to empower themselves!

1

# Empowered to do what?

For organizations, the one type of team where empowerment is particularly important is the *new product (or service) development team.* These teams are usually operating in a competitive marketplace where getting to the market fast with the best product is critical to success.

Let's take a look at some of the decisions that a new product team might be empowered to make:

❶ Defining the technical and business specifications of the potential product.

❷ Determining the content of the product and process design content.

❸ Scheduling and managing the budget.

❹ Obtaining resources such as people, tools, and facilities.

❺ Selecting and coordinating with vendors.

❻ Collaborating with other teams, senior management, and regulatory agencies.

❼ Monitoring progress and evaluating performance.

> "A team really gets empowered after they have made a decision and you support it."
>
> *— Paul Hartley*

# EMPOWERMENT IS NOT...

There is a good deal of misinformation floating around about empowerment. For example:

- ❖ **Empowerment means "hands off."** Some managers and even some team leaders think when a team is empowered, the manager is supposed to do "nothing." This is abandonment.

- ❖ **Empowerment of the team means unempowerment of the manager.** This is also a myth. In an empowered world, the role of the manager changes and grows more complex, but is certainly no less important.

- ❖ **Empowerment means the manager is no longer accountable for results**. Wrong. Empowered teams are a means to an end but, for example, the Vice President of Sales is still responsible for sales results.

- ❖ **Empowerment means the manager plays a more passive role.** This is another myth. When teams in a manager's area are empowered, he or she will need to be active, but in different ways requiring different skills, as will become apparent on the next page.

> "When Nike says, 'Just Do It!' that's a message of empowerment."
>
> — *Naomi Klein*

3

# The Role of the Manager

When teams are empowered, the role of the manager becomes both more necessary and more challenging.

- ❖ **Coach not Control**. In an empowered world, managers help the team see the big picture, look at opportunities, be aware of obstacles and anticipate problems that may arise in the future.

- ❖ **Champion not Command**. The empowered team should not look to the manager to make decisions for them but to be a cheerleader for their work. In fact, when a team comes to the manager for a decision, the manager should turn them back around and insist that they decide.

- ❖ **Advocate not Abdicate**. When opportunities at key business meetings and other forums present themselves, the manager should support the work of the team with senior management, other key stakeholders, support groups, vendors, and others who need to know about the good work of the team.

- ❖ **Teach not Preach**. The effective manager of an empowered team can help the team succeed by providing the team leader and others with the key skills (e.g., negotiations) and knowledge (e.g., market dynamics) that may be needed.

- ❖ **Facilitate not Obfuscate**. The central job of the manager is to make it easier for the team to be successful by providing a motivating goal, clear expectations, and useful knowledge.

> "Managers who empower teams in their area are demonstrating the highest form of respect. It sends a positive and powerful message that says 'I value you.'"
>
> — *Glenn Parker*

4

# EMPOWERMENT: THE BENEFITS

So, what is all the fuss about? How does being an empowered team help the company succeed? And how does having an organization of empowered teams help the business and its bottom line. The goal of empowerment is not just to make team members feel good about themselves, although that does happen as a byproduct. The benefits are more specific and more business-like.

- ❖ **Speed**. Empowered teams speed up the product development process because they do not have to stop and wait for approvals from management before proceeding to the next step. Empowered teams reduce the time it takes to respond to a customer request because they are authorized to provide an answer. The net result: products get to the market faster and customers are happier.

- ❖ **Creativity**. Empowered teams tend to be creative and, as a result, come up with more innovative solutions because the fear of being "second-guessed" or overruled has been eliminated. They are free to brainstorm, to think "outside of the box," and to take a chance on a new idea and be supported by their manager.

- ❖ **Motivation**. Empowered team members are more highly motivated to work hard to achieve team success. One reason is that when you empower a person or group you are sending a strong message of "respect." An empowered person or team is respected to the extent they are being told they are in charge and, therefore, smart enough to make the right choices and decisions for the organization. It's a powerful message.

# EMPOWERMENT: THE DOWNSIDE

With all the positive outcomes from empowered teams, can there be any downside? Can something go wrong? Is it possible that there can be too much of a good thing—too much empowerment?

In their 2000 article in the *Journal of Personal Selling and Sales Management*, Perry, Pearce and Sims point out three areas of concern:

❶ **Overzealousness.** An empowered team may overreach the boundaries of its authority and create problems for other parts of the business. For example, a sales team, in its desire to close a deal, may make promises that result in additional or unwanted work for another department.

❷ **Perceived loss of status for middle managers.** Managers may perceive the empowerment of teams in their area as a decrease in their authority and, therefore, their importance in the organization. As a result, they may refuse to provide coaching or advocacy for the team, or even try to block some team efforts.

❸ **The empowered team as counterculture.** If the primary culture of the organization is top-down, command and control, and silo-driven with no history of empowerment, then an empowered team in an organization may present a threat. However, it also may be seen as the vanguard of something positive in the future.

> "Culture of the mind must be subservient to the heart."
>
> – *Mohandis Gandhi*

6

# LEVELS OF EMPOWERMENT

Some organizations like to use a progression of authority, so that as the team becomes more capable and confident their level of empowerment increases. The levels or continuum usually runs from the manager making all decisions on the one hand to the team making all decisions on the other.

Some years ago, Delta Faucet developed and used six levels of empowerment:

## Six Levels of Empowerment

**Level 1:**  The manager decides

**Level 2:**  The team has increasing input; the manager decides

**Level 3:**  The team recommends; the manager decides

**Level 4:**  The team decides and informs the manager prior to taking action

**Level 5:**  The team decides and implements the decision, then informs the manager

**Level 6:**  The team decides; no further action is required

# Levels of Empowerment: Four Questions

In order for the process of empowerment to be successful, it is important that the team work with management to discuss and decide the degree of authority that will be given to the team. The process needs to go beyond the generalities of "make key decisions" and "provide input" to an agreement on what specific decisions the team will be empowered to make and what decisions will be reserved for management.

A number of years ago, author Fran Rees provided us with four key questions that help move this process along from the general to the specific:

**❶** What decisions will be the *sole responsibility* of the team?

**❷** What decisions will be made *collaboratively* between the team and management?

**❸** What decisions will be reserved *for management* but with team input?

**❹** What decisions will be reserved *for management* but *without* team input?

**Quick Team Exercise:**

❖ Divide the team into four sub-groups.

❖ Ask each group to answer one of the four questions.

❖ After each group reports, facilitate a discussion leading to a consensus for each question.

# EMPOWERMENT: HOW IT WORKS

One of the most famous and successful stories of empowerment concerned AT&T's development of the 4200 cordless phone back in the late 1980s.

> ...cross-functional teams of engineers, manufacturers and marketers were formed with *authority to make every decision on how the product would work, look, be made and cost. The key was to set rigid speed requirements for freezing all specs. Because the team did not need to send each decision up the line for approval, it could meet those strict deadlines.* With this new approach, AT&T cut development time for the 4200 phone from two years to just one year while lowering costs and increasing quality.
>
> – B. Dumaine, *Fortune,* February 13, 1989.

A similar story was told by the Technical Services Division of Parke-Davis Pharmaceuticals.

> The company needed to improve turnaround time on its ability to deliver data management statistics and research to the folks in clinical development. *Empowering the teams to act led to significant decreases in time for deliverables, in some cases up to 75 percent.*
>
> – Glenn Parker, *Cross-Functional Teams,* Jossey-Bass/Wiley, 2003.

"People shape themselves through their decisions."

*– Rene Dubos*

# Empowerment: How It Works

This case represents a different but all too common form of empowered team, where there were clear parameters to the team's actions.

> At a business unit of Telecordia Technologies, a cross-functional team was charged with improving inter-group communication and employee morale. Since cost-containment was an important company priority, *the boundary of the team was defined in dollar terms. Any idea that required a "significant" financial expenditure required approval of the management team. This limitation has an unintended salutary effect since it required members to learn how to prepare and present a business case for each financial request.*

> — Glenn Parker, *Cross-Functional Teams,*
> Jossey-Bass/Wiley, 2003

**Quick Team Exercise:**

1. Ask each member of the team to read the three cases.

2. Divide into three sub-groups.

3. Ask each sub-group to analyze the case to identify:

   ❖ What are the key learnings about empowerment?

   ❖ How can we apply these learnings to our team?

# ROAD MAP TO EMPOWERMENT

Empowerment is not a gift. It is not something you get for your birthday or anniversary. For teams there are a variety of ways to become empowered.

**Empowerment as a company policy**. Some organizations realize that empowered teams are a strategic advantage. As in the AT&T example in the previous section, empowered teams get new products to the market faster, better, and cheaper. And "first to the market" can mean a significant advantage in long-term market share.

**Gradual evolution**. Some teams work their way up the continuum from complete management control through participation in decision-making and finally to being empowered to make all decisions within certain parameters. Along the way they prove themselves to be responsible and capable of making decisions on their own.

**Becoming empowered by acting empowered.** As we often say "ambiguity is an opportunity." When there is lack of clarity about whether your team is empowered to make a decision, some teams simply "go for it." As long as they are not doing anything that is illegal, unethical, or contrary to corporate policy, and it is in the best interests of the customer and the company, it makes sense to empower yourself.

# Roadmap to Empowerment: Your Team Charter

One way to clarify the extent of your team's authority to act and make decisions is to have a discussion with your manager about it. The discussion should center around the boundaries of the team's ability to take action without checking with management. You want to know which decisions are under the team's control, which are reserved for management, and which are decided jointly. You may use the list below to guide your discussion.

**Team Decisions:**

- ❖ Create team goals

- ❖ Assign work

- ❖ Develop our project plan and budget

- ❖ Decide how work will get done

- ❖ Change project or other plans

- ❖ Set standards

- ❖ Communicate with customers, vendors, and others outside of the team

- ❖ Establish a team meeting schedule

- ❖ Make spending decisions.

# EMPOWERED TEAMS ACT EMPOWERED

We see teams taking responsibility and assuming they have the authority to act. They do not wait for management's approval. On the other hand, many people believe they are unempowered because "they" won't let them make important decisions. Who are "they?" They are corporate management, policies, procedures, laws, regulations, etc. Often, this feeling is embedded in the belief system or culture of the organization. As a result, people stop trying. They simply keep their head down, wait to be told what to do, and then do it without question.

When people stop trying to take responsibility, this tends to reinforce management's belief that teams should not be empowered, because team members are not capable of doing things correctly. In turn, management imposes more checks and puts more controls on team's actions.

There is a ripple effect here as people stop believing in their ability to do things well and, as a result, avoid taking responsibility. This lack of self-efficacy (i.e., belief in one's ability) often leads to a feeling of dependency and avoidance of taking on challenges. They don't want to be empowered.

> "I was consumed with the fear of failing. Reaching deep down and finding confidence has made all my dreams come true."
>
> — *A. Hall*

13

# Empowered Teams Act Empowered

In some situations, teams become empowered by simply seeing the opportunity and assuming they have the authority to act. In other situations, teams are empowered by management as a result of discussion and negotiations.

IBM had about 150 customers in the Twin Towers in New York City on September 11, 2001, whose IT infrastructure was badly disrupted as a result of the terrorists' attack on the World Trade Center. The most urgent need was to enable the New York Stock Exchange and the banking industry to return to operation as soon as possible. As Frank Brinkman, co-leader of the IBM post-9/11 team said, "we just *assumed our role* was to get the customer up and running again and we should do whatever it takes to make that happen." They acted as if they were empowered.

At a recent corporate retreat, project team leaders were asked to create three lists: (1) decisions their team is empowered to make; (2) decisions reserved for management; and (3) decisions their team should be empowered to make. The first list only included a few items; the second list was quite long and, surprisingly, the third list contained just a few items. As one project manager told me, "I'm happy just the way it is. We make recommendations to management and they decide." These teams were not ready to be empowered. And it's not likely that management will empower them.

14

# EMPOWERED TEAMS HAVE CLEAR FOCUS

Your team will never be empowered unless you can answer the questions: *For what* or *To do what?* You cannot expect anyone to give you *carte blanche* empowerment like an open line of credit.

You need to be clear about:

- ❖ **Goals:** What are your expected outcomes?

- ❖ **Plans:** How you will achieve your goals?

- ❖ **Benefits:** How will this help the company succeed?

- ❖ **Budgets:** What will it cost?

- ❖ **Measures:** How will we know if we succeeded?

- ❖ **Authority:** Who is empowered to make which decisions?

> "Man is a goal-seeking animal. His life only has meaning if he is reaching out and striving for his goals."
>
> – *Aristotle*

# An Empowerment Plan

Many organizations use a formal process often called a project plan or a statement of work. While the contents may differ slightly, most plans include:

- ❖ Goals

- ❖ Benefits

- ❖ Task or specific action steps

- ❖ Resources required

- ❖ Communication plan and check points

- ❖ Deliverables

- ❖ Timeline

- ❖ Costs

- ❖ Return on investment

- ❖ Decision boundaries

## EMPOWERED TEAMS | ENGAGE KEY STAKEHOLDERS

While empowered teams may have freedom to act, they must do so in concert with key stakeholders both inside and outside the organization. Important stakeholders have the ability to help your team clear a smooth path to success or create obstacles that can make the achievement of your goals extremely difficult.

More than 20 years ago, while the rest of us were focusing on internal team dynamics as key determinants of success, Deborah Ancona and her colleagues at MIT were demonstrating that high-performing teams were engaged in more external activity with key stakeholders during all phases of a project than low-performing teams. Ancona identified three types of engagement with stakeholders:

1. **Scouting.** Working to understand stakeholders' expectations, as well as learning other information about them.

2. **Ambassadorship.** Connecting the team's work to the company strategy and garnering resources and cooperation from others.

3. **Task Coordination.** Managing the interdependencies with other internal and external groups.

For more information, see D. Ancona & H. Bresman, *X-Teams: How to Build Teams That Lead, Innovate and Succeed.* Harvard Business School Press, 2007.

# Worksheet: Engaging Key Stakeholders

1. Identify a key team stakeholder.

   _____

2. What type of help do you need from this stakeholder?

   _____

   _____

   _____

3. What type of help does this stakeholder need from you?

   _____

   _____

   _____

4. What common objectives do you share with this stakeholder?

   _____

   _____

   _____

5. Which member of your team would be the best person to serve as "ambassador"?

   _____

6. What specific steps can you take to develop a positive relationship with this stakeholder?

   _____

   _____

   _____

> "If you live in the river, you should make friends with the crocodile."
>
> — *Indian Proverb*

# EMPOWERED TEAMS ARE COMMITTED

No matter how a team gets empowered, they are usually strongly committed to something. This commitment is especially important for cross-functional teams, where members come from various functional areas, each with their own set of goals and priorities. Most new product and project teams are cross-functional.

In these situations, members need to put aside these often competing priorities and get behind an overarching goal or consuming challenge. It really doesn't matter what team members rally around. It can even be what some might see as a negative goal such as removing the bugs in an existing product, beating the competition to the market, or changing the negative image of the organization.

Rarely will teams generate strong commitment to something like "improving the bottom line" or "increasing shareholder value." However, team members can get behind something like "reducing the negative side effects of_____," or "increasing customer satisfaction."

# Team Commitment

**Purpose:** To identify the things to which your team is committed.

**Process:** Review the list below and identify the most important thing that motivates your team and creates a high level of team member commitment. Discuss your responses with your teammates.

_____ 1. Increasing sales and profits

_____ 2. Beating the competition

_____ 3. Improving the lives of our customers

_____ 4. Achieving a high level of customer satisfaction

_____ 5. Reducing our product costs

_____ 6. Producing a quality product

_____ 7. Increasing our stock price

_____ 8. Achieving a high level of employee satisfaction

_____ 9. Other (please describe)  _____

_____

**Comments:**

> "One of the best kept secrets is that people are aching to make a commitment, if they only had the freedom and environment in which to do so."
>
> *– John Naisbett*

# EMPOWERED TEAMS COMMUNICATE!

More specifically, empowered teams communicate effectively with key stakeholders. Stakeholders—anyone who has a "stake" in the work of the team—often hold the key to the team's continuing ability to function effectively as an empowered team. Effective teams use meeting minutes, project summaries, management presentations, informal conversations and many other tools to keep stakeholders informed and comfortable with the team's ability to get the job done well.

Stakeholders get nervous and wary of the team's decision-making capability when they do not know what is going on. In one study of 53 new product development teams, it was reported that managers tended to withdraw power from teams "when they did not have a shared understanding of their process." When there is no shared understanding and little communication about the direction of the project, managers are more likely to be uncomfortable with the team's ability to make good decisions on their own. The result: managers begin to look more closely at how the team is functioning and start to step in and either check on the team's decisions or actually take them over. This unempowering of the team may not be justified, but it is nevertheless the result of a lack of communication from the team to the stakeholders.

# Communicate with Key Stakeholders

**Process:** Begin by making a list of your key stakeholders. For example, senior management, functional departments managers, support groups, etc. Use their specific name or title (e.g., Vice President, Clinical Development). Then make another list of the communications tools at your disposal (e.g., meeting minutes, staff meeting presentations). Finally, match the stakeholder with the appropriate communication tool(s).

|   | Stakeholder | Best way to communicate: |
|---|---|---|
| 1. | _____ | _____ |
| 2. | _____ | _____ |
| 3. | _____ | _____ |
| 4. | _____ | _____ |
| 5. | _____ | _____ |

> "The road to a friend's house is never long."
>
> *– Danish Proverb*

22

# TEAM MEMBER EMPOWERMENT

We spend so much time focusing on empowering the team to make decisions and take other actions that we often forget to address the very important issue of team member empowerment. Many of the benefits of empowerment discussed earlier require the empowerment of members to act quickly and decisively.

Member empowerment is especially significant for cross-functional or project teams, where members come from many different departments. Members must be able to make decisions and other commitments, accept action items, and generally speak on behalf of their functional area. There is nothing more frustrating than hearing a team member say, "I'll have to check with my manager first" when asked if they are able to support a proposed team decision.

Member empowerment and team empowerment are closely intertwined. Member empowerment supports team empowerment and team empowerment facilitates member empowerment. They are bound together and are key factors in team success.

If members get mixed messages from their manager or the messages are constantly changing, it will be difficult for the team to function as a fully empowered and effective team.

# Team Member Empowerment Factors

1.  **Freedom to make decisions.** Members must be able to actively participate in team discussions leading up to and including the making of a decision.

2.  **Freedom to make commitments**. Members must be able to commit their functional area to work projects and other activities that are needed by the team.

3.  **Freedom to accept work assignments.** Members must be able to accept action items needed by the team, whether it is as simple as getting a copy of an existing report or preparing a new report.

4.  **Communication of department information.** The team often needs current information about relevant activities in a department that may have an impact on the work of the team. Members must be able to be a responsible spokesperson for the department.

5.  **Communication of team information.** Communication goes both ways. The department needs to know about team goals, decisions, and other actions. Functional area managers need to see the member as a trusted communicator of team information.

> "More than anything else, I believe it's our decisions, not the conditions of our lives, that determines our destiny."
>
> — *Tony Robbins*

24

## Team Empowerment Survey

**Directions:** Please read each statement and then indicate the extent to which it is true about your team according to the following scale:

> 1 – Not at all
> 2 – To some extent
> 3 – To a moderate extent
> 4 – To a great extent
> 5 – To a very great extent

_____ 1. Our team has significant influence over the development of our goals and plans.

_____ 2. Our team is empowered to make all decisions that affect our work.

_____ 3. Our team plays a major role in selecting and changing team membership.

_____ 4. Functional department managers do not interfere with our decision-making.

_____ 5. Our team has control over our work assignments.

_____ 6. Team members are empowered to take action on behalf of their functional area without checking with their manager.

_____ 7. Our team is empowered to identify and solve all problems that arise within the scope of our goals.

_____ 8. The team is empowered to do whatever it takes to accomplish the goals and carry out the plan.

_____ **Total**

# Team Empowerment Survey: Scoring

**8 – 16: Dependent.** Teams in this category have little freedom or authority to act in an independent manner. They look to management to tell them what to do and, often, how to do it.

**17 – 31: Participative.** Teams in this range are moving toward self-direction by using a variety of participative tools that involve members in goal-setting and decision-making. However, all plans and major decisions must be approved by management.

**32 – 40: Empowered.** If you are in this range, your team is highly self-directed which is reflected in your freedom to develop goals and plans and then carry out those plans with minimal control by management.

### The Empowerment Continuum: Where is your team?

8 ————————————17————————————32 ———————————— 40

**Note:** After completing and scoring the survey, plot your team on this continuum. Then discuss what you need to do to move toward becoming an empowered team.

# Authority Assessment

**Description:** Here is a quick checkup on the degree of authority which your team exercises.

On *key decisions* that affect the work of your team, how are these decisions made?

❶ Manager decides and informs the team; no input by team members.

❷ Manager asks for input from team members; manager decides.

❸ Manager and team members jointly make the decisions, usually by consensus.

❹ Team is empowered to make the decisions, then inform the manager.

**Discuss the Results:**

1. Ask people for various definitions of "key decisions."
2. Ask for examples of past decisions that fit into one of the four categories.
3. Discuss how the levels of empowerment have impacted the success of the team.
4. What decisions not made by the team now should the team be empowered to make in the future?

# An Empowerment Story

A pharmaceuticals company established a series of cross-functional, "cycle-time reduction teams" to look at ways to reduce the time it takes to get the product to the customer. We were engaged to help the teams work effectively together to accomplish their goals.

At first, each team was told both the number of days the cycle time for their product could be reduced and ways to reduce the time. At one of the first team launch meetings, the team leader asked, "If you are telling us what to do and how to do it, *what do you need us for?*" After some embarrassment, management agreed with the implication of the question and decided to open up the process. They subsequently charged the teams with developing their own reduction target and with providing recommendations on ways to achieve the goal.

It was later discovered that the teams usually came up with more ambitious cycle-time reduction targets than those originally proposed by management!

**What is the point of this story?**

_____

_____

_____

_____

_____

_____

"I have not failed. I have just found 10,000 ways that don't work."

*— Thomas Edison*

# EMPOWERMENT AND RESPECT

*All I'm askin' for is*
*a little respect when you come home (just a little bit)*
*I ain't gonna do you wrong,*
*while you're gone*
*All I'm asking for is*
*a little respect when you come home (just a little bit)*

– "Respect" by Aretha Franklin

You respect people when you empower them. This is the message of a wonderful book simply called *Respect* by Harvard sociologist Sara Lawrence Lightfoot. One of the six people the author profiles in the book, Jennifer, a mid-wife in a clinic, teaches women to be "in charge," to "eliminate the passivity," and to "participate and make choices" about their health care. Jennifer says to the women, "you are problem-solving, learning, asking questions. *You can decide.*" She was teaching them to be empowered!

> "They cannot take away our self-respect if we do not give it to them."
>
> *– Mahatma Gandhi*

# Management and Respect

Managers who empower teams in their area by encouraging and supporting their efforts to make decisions about various aspects of their work are demonstrating the highest form of respect. It sends a powerful message that says, "*I value you.*"

**Discussion Guide**

1. Are some teams in your organization going about their business in a fairly passive manner, waiting to be told what to do? They don't seem to respect themselves and others do not respect them. Why is this happening?

2. On the other hand, are there some teams in your organization that seem to be acting as if they are empowered? As a result, they are these gaining the respect of others in the organization for their mode of operation? Why is this happening? How is the organization benefitting from this?

3. One way to get some teams to become more assertive and in control of their destiny is to empower them. What are some ways you can show your respect for these teams via the empowerment process?

> "If you have respect for people as they are, you can be more effective in helping them to be better than they are."
>
> — *John Gardner*

# FEAR    OF EMPOWERMENT

While many of us would welcome more control over decisions that affect our work, actions taken by our teams, and changes that impact our work environment, others fear empowerment. They fear being held responsible and, therefore, accountable for the results. In a labor market where unemployment is high, jobs requiring your skill set are decreasing, and work is being shipped offshore, it is natural that employees might not welcome the responsibility that comes with empowerment.

Years ago, at one of my clients, members of shop-level teams were told that their "natural work groups" were going to migrate to self-directed, empowered teams over time. Rather than cheer this change that would have moved responsibility for certain key work process decisions to the teams, one outspoken shop steward said (in voicing the concerns of many of his co-workers), "in other words, we'll be held accountable, so if anything goes wrong, we'll get disciplined or fired."

He believed that is what happened to supervisors who made a mistake or a poor decision. In fact, no one at the plant had ever been fired for making a mistake unless it was for doing something reckless such as being drunk on the job.

> "Our deepest fear is not that we are inadequate. Our deepest fear is that we are powerful beyond our measure. It is our light, not our darkness, that frightens us most...As we are liberated from our own fear, our presence automatically liberates others."
>
> *— Nelson Mandela*

31

# Overcoming Fear of Empowerment

## Team Discussion Guide

1. Review the case on the previous page. What do you think was *really* going on in that plant?

2. What are some of factors in the culture of an organization that leads to fear of empowerment?

3. What are some of the factors in the culture of your organization that may lead to a fear of empowerment? What examples have you seen where the "fear factor" has been present?

4. How do you overcome the fear of team empowerment? In overcoming the fear, what role should be played by:

   ❖ Management, including the team sponsor

   ❖ Team leader

   ❖ Team stakeholders, especially the functional area managers

   ❖ Team members

   ❖ Other: _____

# Empowerment Resources

## Books

Bill Ginnodo, *The Power of Empowerment*, Pride Publications, 1997. Includes articles by experts such as William Byham and Susan Mohrman as well as 16 case studes from companies ranging from Marriott, Martin Marietta and Federal Express to USAA, Motorola and AT&T.

Daniel Quinn Mills, *The Empowerment Imperative*, HRD Press, 1994. Using an engaging dialogue style between two employees, the heart of the book is a description of a six-step process for achieving a high-performing empowered organization.

Richard Wellins, William Byham & Jeanne Wilson, *Empowered Teams*, Jossey-Bass, 1991. Using data from a survey of 500 organizations and in-depth research in 28 organizations, the authors provide practical insights into how empowered teams actually work and advice for working through the four stages of building strong teams.

Judith Vogt & Kenneth Murrell, *Empowerment in Organizations*, University Associates, 1999. A classic textbook on empowerment covering all the bases with lots of helpful examples and lists.

## Videos

Blue Sky Video, *Improving Work Systems*, www.blueskyvideo.com. The video describes the change to self-directed white collar teams at IDS Financial Services. It covers the business case that led to the work redesign and formation of empowered teams.

Blue Sky Video, *Redesigning the Work Place for Self-Regulation: The Rohm & Haas Story*, www.blueskyvideo.com. This video focusing on the transition to empowered teams in a blue collar or factory situation that also required the cooperation of labor and management.

# Empowerment Resources

ATS Media, *Improving Performance through Empowerment,*
www.atsmedia.com. The theme of this video is on the manager's
role as well as the advantages to managers of delegating
responsibilities to employees, encouraging employees to explore
new ideas and take advantage of new learning opportunities.

## Handbooks for Facilitators

G. Parker & R. Kropp. *50 Activities for Self-Directed Teams,* HRD
Press, 1994. A loose-leaf binder filled with *reproducible* training
and team building exercises for creating and sustaining
empowered teams.

Team Effectiveness. *Coaching Effectiveness Profile,* HRD Press,
2002. This self-assessment instrument rates the person on
coaching competencies such as listening, empathy and
empowering others.

# How to Get the Most Out of This Booklet

1. **Assess Your Team's Current Level of Empowerment.**

   - Use the *Levels of Empowerment: Four Questions*
     (Page 8)

   - Use the *Team Empowerment Survey* (Pages 25–26)

   - Use the *Authority Assessment* (Page 27)

2. **Develop an Understanding of all aspects of Empowerment.**

   - See E*mpowerment is* (Page 1) and
     *Empowerment is Not* (Page 3)

   - See *Empowerment: How it Works* (Page 9–10)

3. **Help Your Team Develop a Plan**

   - Review *Road Map to Empowerment* (Page 11)

   - Review *Your Team Charter* (Page 12).

   - Review *Worksheet: Engaging Key Stakeholders* (Page 18)

4. **Provide Training and Coaching**

   - Facilitate *Team Commitment* (Page 20)

   - Facilitate *Communicate with Key Stakeholders* (Page 22)

   - Facilitate *Team Empowerment Survey* (Page 25–26)

   - Review *Empowerment Resources* (Pages 33–34)

# Glenn Parker

## Author

As a consultant for more than 30 years, Glenn Parker has helped create high-performance teams at hundreds of organizations including Novartis Pharmaceuticals, Merck & Company, Philips-Van Heusen, Telcordia Technologies, BOC Gases, and the U.S. Coast Guard. He is an internationally-recognized workshop facilitator, organizational consultant, and conference speaker in the areas of teamwork and team meetings.

Glenn is the author of some 16 books including several best-sellers such as *Team Players and Teamwork, Rewarding Teams: Lessons from the Trenches,* and *Cross Functional Teams: Working with Allies, Enemies and Other Strangers;* widely used instruments such as the *Parker Team Player Survey* and manuals for practitioners such as *50 Activities for Team Building, 25 Instruments for Team Building,* and *Team Workout: 50 Interactive Activities.*

His seminal work in team player styles was featured in the best-selling CRM video, *Team Building II: What Makes a Good Team Player?* Glenn is one of only 75 management thinkers recognized in the book, *The Guru Guide.* His latest book, *Meeting Excellence: 33 Tools to Lead Meetings that Get Results,* has been widely quoted and referenced in articles in the *New York Times, Forbes, CIO Magazine,* and others.

Glenn is the father of three grown children and currently lives in the Princeton, New Jersey area with his wife, Judy. In his spare time, he is an active volunteer with the American Cancer Society where he helped create **Run for Dad,** a Father's Day event designed to raise awareness about prostate cancer, which regularly draws thousands of participants.